CONTENTS

go figure

You are an intrepid animal scientist and your job is to use your mathematical knowledge to explore some of the wildest parts of the planet, examining the creatures living there.

Learn about expressions, symmetry, place value and other mathematical principles and then use them to solve puzzles that will guide you while you walk on the wild side.

Answers to the Go Figure! challenges can be found on page 28.

Words in *italics* appear in the glossary on page 30.

WHAT EQUIPMENT DO YOU NEED?

You might find some of the questions in this book are too hard to do without the help of a calculator.
Ask your teacher about when and how to use a calculator.

Pen or pencil

Notepad

Protractor

Ruler

ADDING ANTS!

Your first mission is to find out how much anteaters eat in the South American grasslands. However, an anteater has broken into your stores and some ants have gone missing.

LEARN ABOUT IT

ADDING AND SUBTRACTING

You can *add* and *subtract* numbers with two, three or more digits by lining them up into columns.

04

Stack the numbers, one on top of the other, making sure the units (U), tens (T) and hundreds (H) line up:

$$
\begin{array}{r}
\text{H T U} \\
182 + \\
274 \\
\hline
* * *
\end{array}
$$

ADDING
Add the units column first:
2 + 4 = 6

$$
\begin{array}{r}
182 + \\
274 \\
\hline
* * 6
\end{array}
$$

Then add the tens column. Sometimes the total for a column is more than 10:
8 + 7 = 15
Put the '5' at the bottom of the column and carry over the '1', putting it at the top of the next column:

$$
\begin{array}{r}
1 \\
182 + \\
274 \\
\hline
* 5 6
\end{array}
$$

Add the hundreds column, remembering the carried-over number:

$$
\begin{array}{r}
1 \\
182 + \\
274 \\
\hline
4 5 6
\end{array}
$$

SUBTRACTING

We cannot take '3' from '1'. This time, you can borrow 1 from the tens column and take '3' from '11' leaving '8':

$$
\begin{array}{r}
95\overset{1}{1} - \\
243 \\
\hline
**8
\end{array}
$$

Don't forget to add the '1' back into the next column:

Now we take (4 + 1) from 5 in the tens column: **5 − 5 = 0**

$$
\begin{array}{r}
95\,1 - \\
2\overset{1}{4}3 \\
\hline
*08
\end{array}
$$

Finally, you can subtract the '2' from the '9' in the hundreds column to complete the sum.

$$
\begin{array}{r}
951 - \\
2\overset{1}{4}3 \\
\hline
708
\end{array}
$$

〉GO FIGURE!

You have counted the number of ants left in your storage boxes and written numbers on the sides.

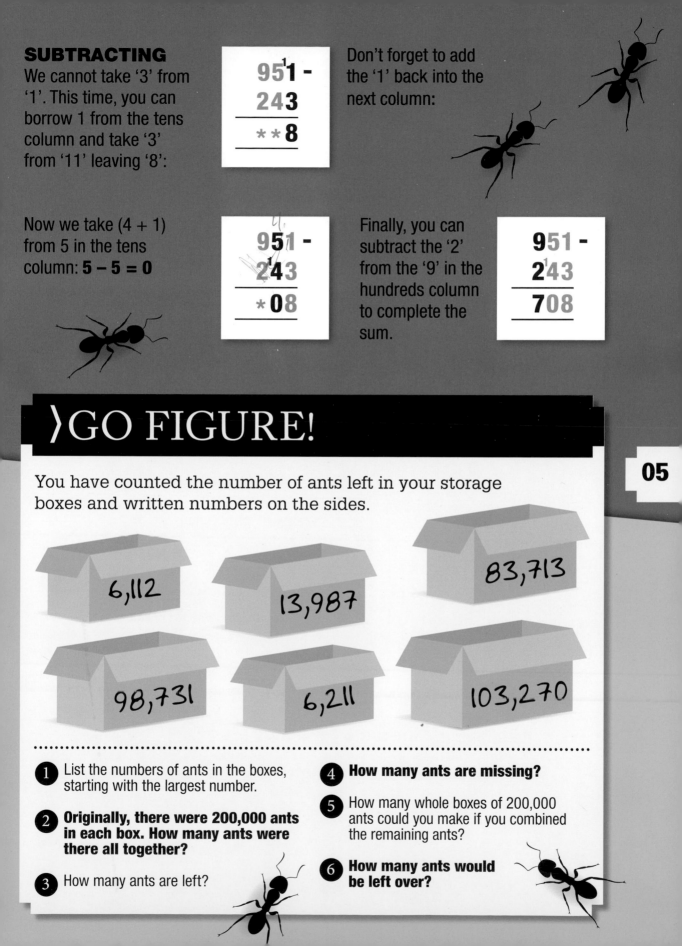

6,112

13,987

83,713

98,731

6,211

103,270

1. List the numbers of ants in the boxes, starting with the largest number.

2. **Originally, there were 200,000 ants in each box. How many ants were there all together?**

3. How many ants are left?

4. **How many ants are missing?**

5. How many whole boxes of 200,000 ants could you make if you combined the remaining ants?

6. **How many ants would be left over?**

QUEST FOR THE JAGUAR

Your next mission takes you to the South American rainforests on the hunt for the jaguar. One has been spotted and your job is to find, track and record the jaguar in action.

LEARN ABOUT IT
PERIMETER AND AREA

The *perimeter* is the distance around the outline of a shape. To work out the perimeter, you have to add up the lengths of all the sides. The *area* of a shape is the space enclosed by it.

To work out the area of a *rectangle*, multiply the length of the short side by the length of the long side. To work out the perimeter of any shape, add up the lengths of all the sides.

5 cm

4 cm

3 cm

2.5 cm

1 cm

7.5 cm

—— **Perimeter is 4 + 5 + 3 + 2.5 + 1 + 7.5 = 23 cm**

Area is made up of 2 rectangles (4 x 5) + (2.5 x 1) = 22.5 cm^2

TIGER SIGHTINGS

You have arrived in India, where you need to track down tigers for research. They are hard to locate, but you have collected details of sightings from local people and plotted them.

LEARN ABOUT IT
QUADRANTS AND COORDINATES

14

A map or plot can be divided into four *quadrants*. You can refer to any point by giving its *coordinates*. The coordinates are two numbers. The first shows the distance you have to go across on the x-*axis*. The second shows the distance you have to go up or down on the y-axis.

Quadrant 2

-3,2

-2,-1

Quadrant 3

Quadrant 1

1,-2

Quadrant 4

y-axis

x-axis

Numbers to the right and above the middle are *positive*.

Coordinates are shown with the x value first. To get from -3,2 to 2,5 you would need to go along 5 and up 3. To get from 1,-2 to -2,-1 you would need to go along -3 and up 1.

Numbers below and to the left of the middle are *negative*.

⟩GO FIGURE!

Your assistant has made a stem-and-leaf plot of the data from the penguin chick survey. Use this to look at the number of chicks at each site.

Number of chicks per nest site:	
stem	leaf
1	8 3
2	9 4 9
3	4 6 7 2
4	5 4 0
5	2 7

1 How many nest sites did you study?

2 **How many sites had between 35 and 60 chicks?**

3 How many chicks were there in total at nests with fewer than 30 chicks?

4 **What is the largest number of chicks at any site?**

5 How many sites had 29 chicks?

6 **What is the total number of chicks in the area?**

ANTARCTICA ANTICS

Travelling to Antarctica, your next task is to monitor penguin populations. You have found beaches with several penguin nest sites and you have counted all the penguin chicks at each site.

12

Stem-and-leaf plots show the frequency of **values** in a set of **data**. They are arranged as a table with two columns.

Each value is split into two digits, one for the tens and one for the units. The stem column shows the tens figure; the leaf column shows the unit figure.

The number 64 is split like this:

stem	leaf
6	4

To record the values 64, 68 and 63, you would fill in the row like this:

stem	leaf
6	4 8 3

This stem-and-leaf plot shows the number of killer whales spotted at five different locations:

Number of killer whales:

stem	leaf
0	8
1	7
2	3 0
3	1

The values recorded were 8 (08), 17, 23, 20 and 31. There are five values in the leaf column because there were five locations.

❯GO FIGURE!

Here are the patterns of the four types of snake living in the area. Only one of them is venomous. To find out which one it is, you need to check the patterns on their bodies.

A

B

C

D

1. A venomous snake has a triangle like this at the end of its tail. The triangle can be reflected on the snake's tail, but not rotated. Which snakes have this feature?

2. **A venomous snake also has a symmetrical pattern along its back. Which snakes have this?**

3. Looking at your answers to questions 1 and 2, only one snake has both the head and body markings that show it is a venomous snake. Which one is it?

4. The snake that bit you had a pattern on its head with rotational symmetry. Which of the four snakes have markings on their heads that have rotational symmetry?

5. Comparing all of your answers, was the snake that bit you venomous?

11

⟩GO FIGURE!

Your assistant has created a map of the area and divided
it into four quadrants, using an x-axis and y-axis. Six tiger
sightings have been made and their coordinates have
been added to the map below.

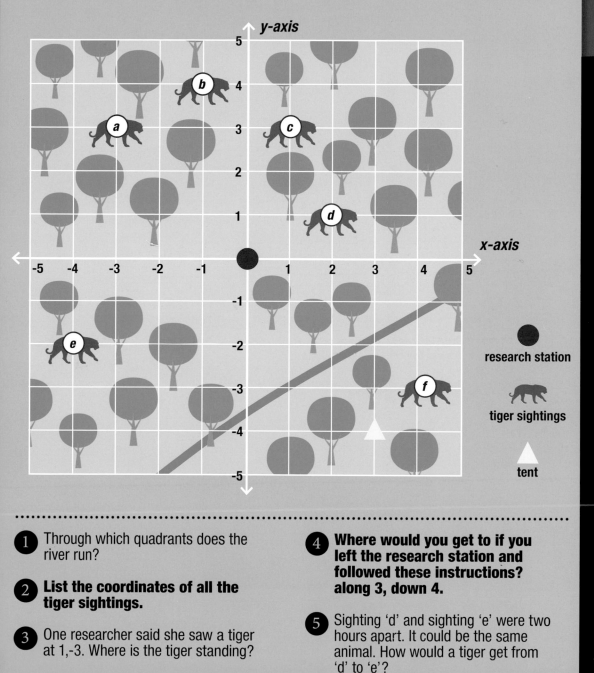

1 Through which quadrants does the
river run?

2 List the coordinates of all the
tiger sightings.

3 One researcher said she saw a tiger
at 1,-3. Where is the tiger standing?

4 Where would you get to if you
left the research station and
followed these instructions?
along 3, down 4.

5 Sighting 'd' and sighting 'e' were two
hours apart. It could be the same
animal. How would a tiger get from
'd' to 'e'?

COUNTING FISH

Your next mission is to calculate the number of fish on a coral reef. You are using a radar fish-counting device, which records the numbers of fish using symbols in columns of units, tens, hundreds, and so on.

We use *place value* to show the number of units, tens, hundreds, thousands and so on, that make up a number. We can break numbers down using place value in columns:

100,000 Hundred thousands	10,000 Ten thousands	1,000 Thousands	100 Hundreds	10 Tens	1 Units
4	1	3	0	6	9

This number is 413,069 – four hundred and thirteen thousand and sixty-nine. We could write it out as this sum:

$$
\begin{array}{r}
400,000 + \\
10,000 \\
3,000 \\
60 \\
9 \\
\hline
413,069 \\
\hline
\end{array}
$$

It is easy to see the place value if we use coloured counters or dots:

100,000 Hundred thousands	10,000 Ten thousands	1,000 Thousands	100 Hundreds	10 Tens	1 Units
••••	•	•••		••• ••• •••	•••• •••• •

⟩GO FIGURE!

You have collected data from two zones on the coral reef,
and your radar device has calculated the total number of
fish in each zone.

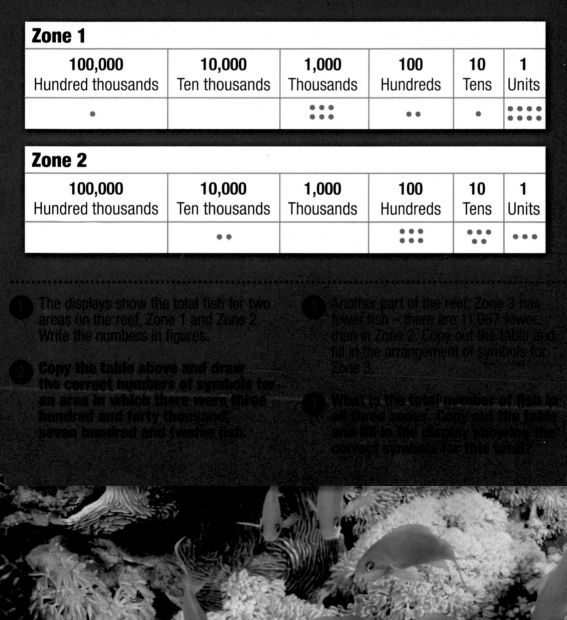

Zone 1

100,000 Hundred thousands	10,000 Ten thousands	1,000 Thousands	100 Hundreds	10 Tens	1 Units
•		⋮⋮⋮	••	•	⋮⋮⋮⋮

Zone 2

100,000 Hundred thousands	10,000 Ten thousands	1,000 Thousands	100 Hundreds	10 Tens	1 Units
	••		⋮⋮⋮•	⋮⋮⋮	•••

1. The displays show the total fish for two
areas on the reef, Zone 1 and Zone 2.
Write the numbers in figures.

2. Copy the table above and draw
the correct numbers of symbols for
an area in which there were three
hundred and forty thousand,
seven hundred and twelve fish.

3. Another part of the reef, Zone 3 has
fewer fish – there are 11,067 fewer
than in Zone 2. Copy out the table and
fill in the arrangement of symbols for
Zone 3.

4. What is the total number of fish in
all three zones. Copy out the table
and fill in the display showing the
correct symbols for this total?

BIRDS OF PARADISE

You have arrived in the jungle of Borneo to study the territories of Birds of Paradise. You have identified three birds, each of which has its own territory.

LEARN ABOUT IT
TRIANGLES

18

There are three types of *triangle*:

A *right-angled* triangle is a special sort of scalene triangle. It has one angle that is 90°.

A scalene triangle has three different sides and three different angles.

The area of a triangle is:
half the base x the height.

The height is a line drawn at right angles to the base up to the opposite corner.

An isosceles triangle has two equal sides and two equal angles.

An equilateral triangle has three equal angles and three equal sides.

Sometimes, the height line has to be drawn outside the triangle.

A 7 cm 6 cm

B 7 cm 4 cm

The area of A is ½ x 6 = 3 x 7 = 21 cm²
The area of B is ½ x 4 = 2 x 7 = 14 cm²

The perimeter of a triangle is the sum of its three sides.

〉GO FIGURE!

You have created a map of the three territories and the triangles they form. Your assistant has also been able to measure the sides of one of the territories.

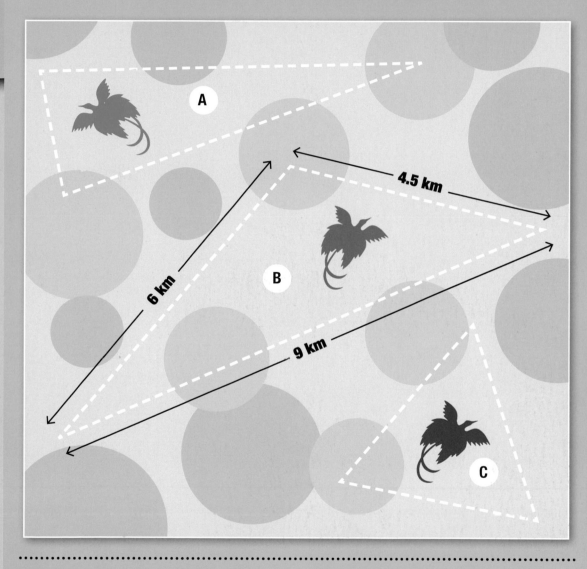

1. Using your ruler, measure the sides of the territories to find out which one is an isosceles triangle?

2. Which territory has three sides of the same length? What is this type of triangle called?

3. Using a protractor to measure the angles, which territory has an angle of 20 degrees?

4. What is the total length of the three sides of Territory B?

TRACKING SEA TURTLES

You have caught two sea turtles and fitted them with tracking devices. You then let the turtles go in the sea and record where they travel over a 24-hour period.

LEARN ABOUT IT
POLYGONS

A *polygon* is a closed shape with straight edges. There are no gaps in its outline. It has corners wherever the edges meet.

Polygon (straight sides)　　**Not a polygon (curved side)**　　**Not a polygon (open)**

Polygons can be regular or irregular. In a regular polygon, all the sides are the same length and all the angles are equal. Examples of regular polygons are: equilateral triangle, square, regular pentagon, regular hexagon, regular octagon.

3 — Equilateral triangle
4 — Square
5 — Regular pentagon
6 — Regular hexagon
8 — Regular octagon

Polygons can have *acute angles*, *obtuse angles* or right-angles. A right-angle is exactly 90°. An obtuse angle is more than 90°. An acute angle is less than 90°.

right angle

obtuse angle (greater than a right angle)

acute angle (less than a right angle)

⟩GO FIGURE!

The tracks of the turtles' routes over the last 24 hours are shown on the map below. Each track is made up of a series of straight parts and angles.

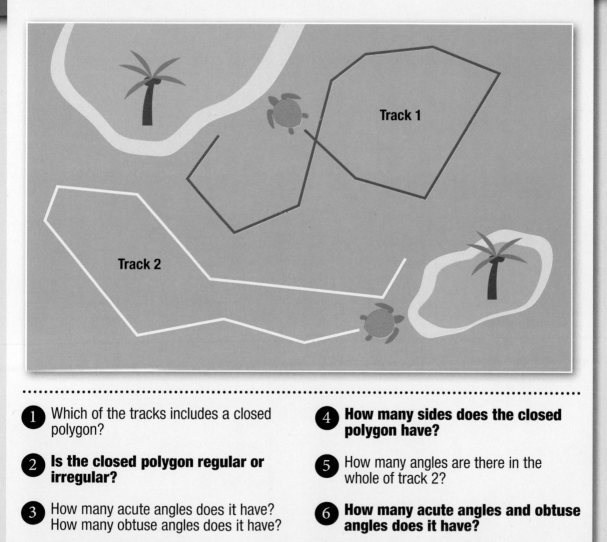

Track 1

Track 2

1. Which of the tracks includes a closed polygon?

2. **Is the closed polygon regular or irregular?**

3. How many acute angles does it have? How many obtuse angles does it have?

4. **How many sides does the closed polygon have?**

5. How many angles are there in the whole of track 2?

6. **How many acute angles and obtuse angles does it have?**

ON THE SAVANNAH

On the African savannah, you have placed video cameras in an area where elephants are known to live. You have used footage of the elephants to calculate their movements.

LEARN ABOUT IT
WORKING WITH TABLES

A *table* is made of boxes, or *cells*, arranged in rows (across the page) and columns (down the page).

When you are using data in a table, you might have to look in all the cells to find the biggest or smallest values, or you might have to do calculations using the numbers in the cells. For example, this may involve adding up all the numbers in a column.

	Rhinos	Zebras	Giraffes
Area 1	11	14	7
Area 2	12	9	3

10   **23**   **23**

From this table, we can see that Area 1 has more animals than Area 2. We can work out that there are 23 rhinos, 23 zebras and 10 giraffes in total.

⟩GO FIGURE!

Information from two video cameras has been used to compile a table. The table shows how many elephants passed by during each period, and the biggest number of elephants that were in shot at any one time during each time period.

TIME	CAMERA 1		CAMERA 2	
	NUMBER OF SIGHTINGS	MOST IN SHOT	NUMBER OF SIGHTINGS	MOST IN SHOT
Midnight–4 am	4	1	5	3
4 am–8 am	7	2	10	4
8 am–12 noon	32	7	45	12
12 noon–4 pm	36	10	53	11
4 pm–8 pm	28	6	23	7
8 pm–midnight	12	3	16	2

1 During which time period were elephants most active?

2 **Which camera was placed in the area with fewest elephant movements?**

3 Looking at the results under 'Most in shot', what is the number that completes this phrase: "There must be at least __ elephants in the area covered by camera 2."

4 **Is it possible to tell how many elephants live in the area just from this data?**

BREEDING MEERKATS

Still in Africa, you move on to study meerkat family groups. You have learned that most meerkat pairs have litters of three babies. This means a meerkat family usually has five members.

LEARN ABOUT IT
MULTIPLICATION PROPERTIES

When you multiply two numbers together, the order of the numbers doesn't matter. This means that:

3 x 4 = 4 x 3

This is called the *commutative property* of multiplication.

When you multiply three or more numbers together, it does not matter in which order you multiply them. This means that

3 x 4 x 5   can be worked out as

3 x 4 = 12
then
12 x 5 = 60

or as

4 x 5 = 20
then
3 x 20 = 60

or as

3 x 5 = 15
then
4 x 15 = 60

This is called the *associative property* of multiplication.

The third property of multiplication is called the *distributive property*. This is because you can distribute or split up numbers into their separate parts. For example:

| 26 x 6 | Can be written as | (20 x 6) + (6 x 6) | or | 120 + 36 = 156 |

❭GO FIGURE!

You are studying two zones to calculate the meerkat population in each. Zone A has an area of 7 km², and Zone B has an area of 9 km². There are three meerkat families for every 1 km².

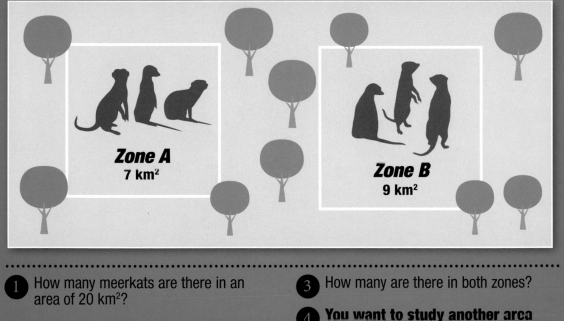

Zone A
7 km²

Zone B
9 km²

1. How many meerkats are there in an area of 20 km²?

2. **You think the number of meerkats in both areas together is (5 x 3 x 7) + (5 x 3 x 9). Your assistant says there is a shorter way of writing this. How would she write this expression, without completing the sum? Which property of multiplication do you have to use?**

3. How many are there in both zones?

4. **You want to study another area that is much larger – 97 km². Round this area up and estimate the number of meerkats.**

5. In this new area, there are two families of elephants, each with four members, for every 1 km². Use the rounded value and estimate the total population.

BUG
POPULATIONS

You are in the rainforests of Central Africa, where you have been finding out about the bug population. You have recorded your travel costs observations in tables.

LEARN ABOUT IT

WORKING WITH TIME AND TABLES

Tables are great ways to study data from different sources. Arranging data in columns allows the figures to be added and compared quickly.

26

TRANSPORT LOG

MONTH 1	£1,983.67
MONTH 2	£978.11
MONTH 3	£2,034.52
MONTH 4	£1,327.88
TOTAL	£

SCORPION STUDIES

POPULATIONS	
ZONE 1	853
ZONE 2	
ZONE 3	694
TOTAL	2,259

After taking your tent down, it rained and some of your records have been smudged. You will have to work out some of the entries.

OBSERVATION LOG

	START	END	TOTAL TIME
MONDAY	▓	13:31	4 HOURS 14 MINS
TUESDAY	09:16	12:58	▓
WEDNESDAY	▓	13:03	4 HOURS 6 MINS
THURSDAY	7:29	▓	8 HOURS 38 MINS

SPIDER OBSERVATIONS

AREA 1	▓
AREA 2	▓
AREA 3	359
TOTAL	▓

1. Look at the transport log. How much of the budget was spent on transport. Write this down in your notebook.

2. **What is the missing number in the scorpion studies list?**

3. What are the numbers that have been smudged in the observation log?

4. **Your assistant is planning research into spiders. She has kept records of the spiders there are in three areas, but the notes are smudged.**

She tells you 'I think there are two hundred and thirty-seven in Area 1 and a hundred and nineteen in Area 2'. Copy out the table and add the missing numbers to complete it.

GO FIGURE! ANSWERS

04-05 Adding ants!
1. 103,270; 98,731; 83,713; 13,987;
   6,211; 6,112
2. 6 x 200,000 = 1,200,000
3. 103,270 + 98,731 + 83,713 + 13,987 +
   6,211 + 6,112 = 312,024
4. 1,200,000 - 312,024 = 887,976
5. Four boxes (800,000 ants)
6. 887,976 - 800,000 = 87,976 ants left

06-07 Quest for the jaguar
1. Zone 1 is a rectangle.
   Its area is 3 km x 5 km = 15 km²
2. The area of Zone 2 is the sum of the
   area of the rectangle and the area of
   the square
   (3.5 km x 4 km) + (2 km x 2 km) =
   14 km² + 4 km² = 18 km²
3. The perimeter of Zone 1 is:
   3 + 5 + 3 + 5 = 16 km
   The perimeter of Zone 2 is:
   4 + 3.5 + 2 + 2 + 2 + 5.5 = 19 km
   So the total perimeter is:
   16 + 19 = 35 km
4. The survey will cost 80 x the total
   area of the two zones:
   80 x (15 + 18) = 80 x 33 = £2,640
5. You need to use 2 cameras for each
   km of perimeter: 19 x 2 = 38 cameras

28

08-09 Foxes and hares
1. 5h
2. 5h = 5 x 180 = 900 hares in 5 km²
3. 4f
4. 4f + 180 = 200 OR 200 − 4f = 180
   OR 200 − 180 = 4f
5. 4f = 20, so f = 5;
   there are 5 foxes in the area

10-11 Snake bite!
1. A, B, D
2. A and C
3. A
4. B, C, D
5. No. Snake A is the only snake that is
   venomous and the markings on its
   head do not have rotational symmetry.

12-13 Antarctica antics
1. 14 sites – there are 14 values in the
   leaf column
2. 7: with values 36, 37, 40, 44, 45, 52, 57
3. 18 + 13 + 29 + 24 + 29 = 113
4. 57
5. 2
6. 18 + 13 + 29 + 24 + 29 + 34 + 36 + 37
   + 32 + 45 + 44 + 40 + 52 + 57 = 490

14-15 Tiger sightings
1. 3 and 4
2. a = -3,3; b = -1,4; c = 1,3; d = 2,1;
e = -4,-2; f = 4,-3
3. The tiger is in the river
4. A tent
5. along -6, down 3

16-17 Counting fish
1. Zone 1: 106,218; Zone 2: 20,653

2.

100,000 Hundred thousands	10,000 Ten thousands	1,000 Thousands	100 Hundreds	10 Tens	1 Units
• • •	• • • •		•••••	•	• •

3. 20,653 − 11,067 = 9,586

100,000 Hundred thousands	10,000 Ten thousands	1,000 Thousands	100 Hundreds	10 Tens	1 Units
		•••••	•••	•••••	••••

4. 106,218 + 20,653 + 9,586 = 136,457

100,000 Hundred thousands	10,000 Ten thousands	1,000 Thousands	100 Hundreds	10 Tens	1 Units
•	• • •	••••	••••	•••	•••••

18-19 Birds of Paradise
1. A
2. C; equilateral
3. A
4. 9 + 6 + 4.5 = 19.5 km

20-21 Tracking sea turtles
1. Track 1
2. Irregular
3. 1 acute, 6 obtuse
4. 7
5. 8
6. 0 acute, 8 obtuse

22-23 On the savannah
1. 12 noon-4pm: 36 + 53 = 89 sightings
2. Camera 1 with a total of 119 sightings
(camera 2 had 152 sightings)
3. 12 – at one point between 8 am-
12 noon there were at least
12 elephants in shot on camera 2,
therefore there must be at least
12 elephants in that area
4. No

24-25 Breeding meerkats
1. 20 km^2 x 3 families x 5 meerkats
per family = 300
2. 5 x 3 x 16. Distributive
3. 5 x 3 x 16 = 240
4. There are 3 x 5 = 15 meerkats in
1 km^2, so an estimate would be
15 x 100 = 1,500 meerkats
5. 2 families x 4 elephants x 100 =
approximately 800 elephants

26-27 Bug populations
1. £6,324.18
2. 2,259 − (853 + 694) = 712
3.

	START	END	TOTAL TIME
MONDAY	09:17	13:31	4 HOURS 14 MINS
TUESDAY	09:16	12:58	3 HOURS 42 MINS
WEDNESDAY	08:57	13:03	4 HOURS 6 MINS
THURSDAY	7:29	16:07	8 HOURS 38 MINS

4.

AREA 1	237
AREA 2	119
AREA 3	359
TOTAL	715

MATHS GLOSSARY

ACUTE ANGLE
An angle that is less than 90°.

ADD
Combining two numbers to produce a third. If two positive numbers are added, then the resulting number will be bigger.

AREA
The amount of two-dimensional space covered by a shape or object. For example, the area of a rectangle is calculated by multiplying the length of one of the short sides by the length of one of the long sides.

ASSOCIATIVE PROPERTY
The associative property of multiplication means that you can multiply sub-groups in a multiplication sum in any order and the answer will remain the same.

AXIS
A line that is used in maths to locate a point.

CELL
A box in a table into which data and numbers are written.

COMMUTATIVE PROPERTY
The commutative property of multiplication means that you can swap numbers around in a multiplication sum and the answer will remain the same.

COORDINATES
A series of numbers that will locate a point against axes.

DATA
A collection of facts or information.

DISTRIBUTIVE PROPERTY
The distributive property of multiplication means that you can split up numbers into their separate parts in a multiplication sum and the answer stays the same.

EQUATION
An expression that can be solved. An equation has two sides to it that are linked with an equals symbol, or another symbol to show an inequality between the two sides.

EXPRESSION
A way of showing the relationship between two amounts.

NEGATIVE NUMBER
A number that is less than zero.

OBTUSE ANGLE
An angle that is more than 90°.

PERIMETER
The total distance around a shape.

PLACE VALUE
The position of a digit within a number

which defines its value. For example, a three digit number has, from right to left, units, tens and hundreds.

POLYGON
A shape that has three or more sides.

POSITIVE NUMBER
A number that is greater than zero.

QUADRANT
One of the four sections created when a shape is divided by two lines that cross, such as the x-axis and y-axis.

RECTANGLE
A four-sided shape where two sides are longer than the other two and all four corners have an angle of 90°.

RIGHT ANGLE
An angle of 90°.

ROTATIONAL SYMMETRY
A object or shape has rotational symmetry when it can be rotated around a point and it still looks the same.

STEM-AND-LEAF PLOT
A way of showing information and values in different sets. Figures are divided into two columns with the left-hand column containing the stems and the right-hand column containing the leafs.

SUBTRACT
Taking one number away from another to produce a third. If a positive number is subtracted from another positive number, then the resulting number will be smaller.

SYMMETRICAL
When a shape or object has parts that are the same when they are reflected or rotated.

TABLE
A way of laying out numbers and information in rows and columns.

TRIANGLE
A shape with three sides. There are three types of triangle. An equilateral triangle has all three sides and angles the same. An isosceles has two of its sides and angles the same. A scalene triangle has all three sides and angles that are different.

VALUE
The total amount that a number or group of numbers adds up to.

VARIABLE
Something that can have a range of possible values. Variables are usually shown in expressions or equations using a letter or other symbol.

INDEX

WEBSITES

www.mathisfun.com

A huge website packed full of explanations, examples, games, puzzles, activities, worksheets and teacher resources for all age levels.

www.bbc.co.uk/bitesize

The revision section of the BBC website, it contains tips and easy-to-follow instructions on all subjects, including maths, as well as games and activities.

www.mathplayground.com

An action-packed website with maths games, mathematical word problems, worksheets, puzzles and videos.

ACKNOWLEDGEMENTS

First published in 2014 by Wayland
Copyright © Wayland 2014

Wayland
338 Euston Road
London NW1 3BH

Wayland Australia
Level 17/207 Kent Street
Sydney NSW 2000
All rights reserved.

Commissioning editor: Debbie Foy

Produced by Tall Tree Ltd
Editors: Jon Richards
Designer: Ed Simkins
Consultant: Steve Winney

ISBN: 9780750282406

Dewey ref: 510-dc23

10 9 8 7 6 5 4 3 2 1

Printed in China
Wayland is a division of Hachette
Children's Books, an Hachette UK company.
www.hachette.co.uk

The website addresses (URLs) included in this book were valid at the time of going to press. However, it is possible that contents or addresses may have changed since the publication of this book. No responsibility for any such changes can be accepted by either the author or the Publisher.

Picture credits
2-3 Shutterstock.com/Inga Nielsen, 4tl Shutterstock.com/Eric Isselee, 9 Shutterstock.com/bikeriderlondon, 10tl Shutterstock.com/Audrey Snider-Bell, 10b all Shutterstock.com/Eric Isselee, 12tl Shutterstock.com/bikeriderlondon, 13 Shutterstock.com/Rich Lindie, 14t and 30bl Shutterstock.com/defpicture, 16 all Shutterstock/serg_dibrova, 17 Shutterstock.com/Rich Carey, 18tr Shutterstock.com/szefei, 20tr Shutterstock.com/Rich Carey, 22tl Shutterstock.com/Patryk Kosmider, 23 Shutterstock.com/Galyna Andrushko, 24 Shutterstock.com/Aaron Amat, 26 and 27 Shutterstock.com/Shutter_M, 26tl Shutterstock.com/Kesu, 26c and b Shutterstock.com/Mikhail Melnikov, 26cb Shutterstock/Aleksey Stemmer, 27cl and cb and 31b Shutterstock.com/Papik